Reformation
GUIDE TO SCRIPTURE

A
Reformation
GUIDE TO SCRIPTURE

THE PROLOGUES FROM THE

GENEVA BIBLE
1560

THE BANNER OF TRUTH TRUST

THE BANNER OF TRUTH TRUST
3 Murrayfield Road, Edinburgh, EH12 6EL, UK
P.O. Box 621, Carlisle, PA 17013, USA

❧

The Geneva Bible first published 1560
This Banner of Truth Trust edition of the
Prologues first published 2010

ISBN-13: 978 1 84871 091 7

❧

❧

Typeset in 10.5/13.5 pt Adobe Caslon Pro at
The Banner of Truth Trust, Edinburgh

Printed in the USA by
Versa Press, Inc.
East Peoria, IL

Contents

Introduction   vii

Epistle Dedicatory to Queen Elizabeth I   ix

To the Brethren of England, Scotland, Ireland, etc.   xix

The Prologues   1

Introduction

THE Geneva Bible of 1560 was the work of a group of English Protestant scholars, living in exile in the city of Geneva during the reign of Mary Tudor (1553–8). They included William Whittingham, Miles Coverdale, Christopher Goodman, Anthony Gilby, Thomas Sampson, and William Cole. The Scottish Reformer John Knox, minister of the English-speaking congregation in the city, may also have had a hand in the translation work.

In their letter to the reader, 'To our beloved in the Lord' (p. xxi–xxiii below), the translators explain what motivated them to undertake the work. Because of the importance of believing and obeying the Word of God, they thought that they could bestow their 'labours and study in nothing which could be more acceptable to God and comfortable to his church than in the translating of the Holy Scriptures into our native tongue'. Accordingly they had been, with 'fear and trembling . . . for the space of two years and more, day and night occupied herein'.

Before the work was ready for publication, Queen Mary died and was succeeded by her half-sister, Elizabeth. The persecution of Protestants ceased, and there seemed to be a golden opportunity to advance the Reformation of the

English church, according to the Word of God. This explains the Epistle Dedicatory addressed to the new Queen (pp. ix–xx below), urging her to do what she could 'to build up the ruins of God's house [the church in England] to his glory, the discharge of [her] conscience, and the comfort of all them that love the coming of Christ Jesus our Lord'.

The new translation immediately became immensely popular, eventually going through more than 150 editions. It was the first Bible printed in Scotland, and was the version later taken to America by the Mayflower Pilgrims. Its influence in the spread of true biblical Christianity throughout the earth is incalculable. Part of the reason for its popularity was the number of study aids it provided, including introductions to each book, cross-references, chapter headings, marginal notes, maps, and tables.

The Trust is marking the 450th anniversary of the first edition by publishing this collection of introductions or prologues to each book of Scripture from the Geneva Bible.[1] It is sent out with the prayer that the prologues will help the reader to see the scope of each book and taste 'the riches of true knowledge and heavenly wisdom' which the Geneva translators found there. The translators' closing advice to the reader of Scripture may also bear repeating: 'Read diligently, judge soberly, and call earnestly to God for the true understanding hereof' (p. 128).

THE PUBLISHER
July 2010

---

[1] We have updated spelling and punctuation, broken down longer sections into paragraphs, added footnotes to clarify obscure words and occasionally added words [in square brackets] to make the meaning clearer. The added footnotes are marked '(Ed.)' to distinguish them from the original footnotes.

TO THE MOST VIRTUOUS AND NOBLE

QUEEN ELIZABETH,

QUEEN OF ENGLAND, FRANCE,
AND IRELAND, &c.

Your humble subjects of the English Church at Geneva
wish grace and peace from God the Father
through Christ Jesus our Lord.

H OW hard a thing it is, and what great impediments let [hinder] to enterprise any worthy act, not only daily experience sufficiently shows (most noble and virtuous Queen), but also that notable proverb confirms the same, which admonishes us that all things are hard which are fair and excellent. And what exercise can there be of greater importance, and more acceptable unto God, or more worthy of singular commendation, than the building of the Lord's temple, the house of God, the church of Christ, whereof the Son of God is the head and perfection?

1 Cor. 3:17
1 Tim. 3:15
Eph. 1:22
Heb. 3:6

When Zerubbabel went about to build the material temple, according to the commandment of the Lord, what difficulties and stays [delays] daily

Ezra 4

arose to hinder his worthy endeavours, the books of Ezra and Esdras [in the Apocrypha] plainly witness; how that not only he and the people of *1 Esdr.* 2:16 God were sore molested with foreign adversaries, *Ezra* 4:6 (whereof some maliciously warred against them, and corrupted the king's officers, and others *Ezra* 4:2 craftily practised under pretence of religion) but also at home with domestical enemies, as *Neh.* 6:10 false prophets, crafty worldlings, faint-hearted *Neh.* 6:18 soldiers, and oppressors of their brethren, who as *Neh.* 5:1 well by false doctrine and lies as by subtle counsel, cowardice, and extortion, discouraged the hearts almost of all, so that the Lord's work was *John* 2:20 not only interrupted and left off for a long time, but scarcely at the length with great labour and *Ezra* 3:12 danger after a sort brought to pass.

Which thing when we weigh aright, and consider earnestly how much greater charge God has laid upon you in making you a builder of his spiritual temple, we cannot but partly fear, *2 Cor.* 2:11 knowing the craft and force of Satan our spiritual enemy, and the weakness and inability of this our nature; and partly be fervent in our prayers toward God that he would bring to perfection this noble work which he has begun by you; and therefore we endeavour ourselves by all means to aid, and to bestow our whole force under your grace's standard, whom God has made as our Zerubbabel for the erecting of this most excellent temple, and to plant and maintain his holy

Word to the advancement of his glory, for your own honour and salvation of your soul, and for the singular comfort of that great flock which Christ Jesus the great Shepherd has bought with his precious blood, and committed unto your charge to be fed both in body and soul.

Heb. 13:20
1 Pet. 1:19

Considering therefore how many enemies there are which by one means or other, as the adversaries of Judah and Benjamin went about to stay the building of that temple, so labour to hinder the course of this building (whereof some are Papists who, under pretence of favouring God's Word, traitorously seek to erect idolatry and to destroy your Majesty, some are worldlings, who as Demas have forsaken Christ for the love of this world; others are ambitious prelates, who as Amaziah and Diotrephes can abide none but themselves; and as Demetrius many practise sedition to maintain their errors) we persuaded ourselves that there was no way so expedient and necessary for the preservation of the one, and the destruction of the other, as to present unto your Majesty the Holy Scriptures faithfully and plainly translated according to the languages wherein they were first written by the Holy Ghost. For the Word of God is an evident token of God's love and our assurance of his defence, wheresoever it is obediently received; it is the trial of the spirits; and as the prophet says, It is as a fire and hammer to break the stony

The enemies which labour to stay religion.
Ezra 4:1

2 Tim. 4:10

Amos 7:12
3 John 9
Acts 19:24

The necessity of God's Word for the reforming of religion.
John 14:23

1 John 4:1
Jer. 23:29

hearts of them that resist God's mercies offered by the preaching of the same. Yea, it is sharper than any two-edged sword to examine the very thoughts and to judge the affections of the heart, and to discover whatsoever lies hid under hypocrisy and would be secret from the face of God and his church. So that this must be the first foundation and groundwork, according whereunto the good stones of this building must be framed, and the evil tried out and rejected.

Heb. 4:12

The ground of true religion.

Now as he that goes about to lay a foundation surely first takes away such impediments as might justly either hurt, let or deform the work, so it is necessary that your Grace's zeal appear herein, that neither the crafty persuasion of man, neither worldly policy, or natural fear dissuade you to root out, cut down and destroy these weeds and impediments which do not only deface your building, but utterly endeavour, yea and threaten, the ruin thereof. For when the noble Josiah enterprised the like kind of work, among other notable and many things he destroyed, not only with utter confusion the idols with their appurtenances, but also burnt (in sign of detestation) the idolatrous priests' bones upon their altars, and put to death false prophets and sorcerers, to perform the words of the law of God; and therefore the Lord gave him good success and blessed him wonderfully, so long as he made God's Word his line and rule to follow,

All impediments must be taken away.

2 Kings 23:16, *2 Chron.* 34:5
Josiah's zeal and true obedience to God.

Deut. 13:5
Lev. 20:6
Deut. 18:11

and enterprised nothing before he had inquired at the mouth of the Lord.

2 Chron. 35:22

And if their zealous beginnings seem dangerous and to breed disquietness in your dominions, yet by the story of king Asa it is manifest that the quietness and peace of kingdoms stands in the utter abolishing of idolatry, and in advancing of true religion; for in his days Judah lived in rest and quietness for the space of five and thirty years, till at length he began to be cold in the zeal of the Lord, feared the power of man, imprisoned the prophet of God, and oppressed the people: then the Lord sent him wars, and at length took him away by death.

2 Chron. 14:5 & 15:15

Wherein stands the quietness of kingdoms.

2 Chron. 16

Wherefore great wisdom, not worldly but heavenly, is here required, which your Grace must earnestly crave of the Lord, as did Solomon, to whom God gave an understanding heart to judge his people aright, and to discern between good and bad. For if God for the furnishing of the old temple gave the Spirit of wisdom and understanding to them that should be the workmen thereof, as to Bezaleel, Aholiab, and Hiram, how much more will he endue your Grace and other godly princes and chief governors with a principal Spirit, that you may procure and command things necessary for this most holy temple, foresee and take heed of things that might hinder it, and abolish and destroy whatever might impair and overthrow the same?

What wisdom is requisite for the establishing of religion and the means to obtain it.

1 Kings 3:9 *2 Chron.* 1:10 *Exod.* 31:1 *1 Kings* 7:14

Diligence and zeal are necessary to build it speedily. *2 Chron.* 34:21, 31

Moreover the miraculous diligence and zeal of Jehoshaphat, Josiah, and Hezekiah are by the singular providence of God left as an example to all godly rulers to reform their countries and to establish the Word of God with all speed, lest the wrath of the Lord fall upon them for the neglecting thereof. For these excellent kings did not only embrace the Word promptly and joyfully, but also procured earnestly and commanded the same to be taught, preached and maintained through all their countries and dominions, binding them and all their subjects both great and small with solemn protestations and covenants before God to obey the Word, and to walk after the ways of the Lord. Yea and in the days of King Asa it was enacted that whosoever would not seek the Lord God of Israel should be slain, whether he were small or great, man or woman. And for the establishing hereof and performance of this solemn oath, as well priests as judges were appointed and placed through all the cities of Judah to instruct the people in the true knowledge and fear of God, and to minister justice according to the Word, knowing that, except God by his Word did reign in the hearts and souls, all man's diligence and endeavours were of none effect: for without this Word we cannot discern between justice and injury, protection and oppression, wisdom and foolishness, knowledge and ignorance, good and evil.

A solemn oath for the maintenance of God's Word. *2 Chron.* 15:13. An act against them that obeyed not God's Word. *2 Chron.* 17:7 & 19:5

What policy must be used for the planting of religion. *Deut*. 6:6 & 18:9

God's Word must go before, or else we build in vain.

Therefore the Lord, who is the chief governor of his church, wills that nothing be attempted before we have inquired thereof at his mouth. For seeing he is our God, of duty we must give him this pre-eminence, that of ourselves we enterprise nothing but that which he has appointed, who only knows all things, and governs them as may best serve to his glory and our salvation. We ought not therefore to prevent [go before] him, or do any thing without his Word, but as soon as he has revealed his will, immediately to put it in execution.

We must first consult with God.
Isa. 30:2

Now as concerning the manner of this building, it is not according to man, nor after the wisdom of the flesh, but of the Spirit, and according to the Word of God, whose ways are diverse from man's ways. For if it was not lawful for Moses to build the material tabernacle after any other sort than God had showed him by a pattern, neither to prescribe any other ceremonies and laws than such as the Lord had expressly commanded, how can it be lawful to proceed in this spiritual building any other ways, than Jesus Christ the Son of God, who is both the foundation, head and chief cornerstone thereof, has commanded by his Word? And forasmuch as he has established and left an order in his church for the building up of his body, appointing some to be apostles, some prophets, others evangelists, some pastors, and teachers, he signifies that

The manner of building is as God has prescribed by his Word.
Isa. 55:8
Exod. 25:4
Acts 7:44
Heb. 8:5
Deut. 5:32

Eph. 4:11

Of whom we must enquire concerning the will of the Lord and knowledge of his Word.

Jer. 15:19
Exod. 4:12
Mal. 2:7
Judg. 1:1
& 20:1
1 Sam.
10:22, 9:9
2 Kings 22:13
*Exod.*28:30

every one, according as he is placed in this body which is the church, ought to enquire of his ministers concerning the will of the Lord, which is revealed in his Word. For they are, says Jeremiah, as the mouth of the Lord: yea he promises to be with their mouth, and that their lips shall keep knowledge, and that the truth and the law shall be in their mouth. For it is their office chiefly to understand the Scriptures and teach them. For this cause the people of Israel in matters of difficulty used to ask the Lord either by the prophets, or by the means of the High Priest, who bare Urim and Thummim, which were tokens of light and knowledge, of holiness and perfection which should be in the High Priest.

What is requisite in them that must give counsel by God's Word.

Therefore when Jehoshaphat took this order in the church of Israel, he appointed Amariah to be the chief concerning the Word of God, because he was more expert in the law of the Lord, and could give counsel and govern according unto the same. Else there is no degree or office which may have that authority and privilege to decise [determine] concerning God's Word, except withal he has the Spirit of God, and sufficient knowledge and judgment to define according thereunto. And as everyone is endued of God with greater gifts, so ought he to be herein chiefly heard, or at least that without the express Word none be heard; for he that has not the Word speaks not by the mouth of the Lord.

Jer. 23:16

Again, what danger it is to do anything, seem it never so godly or necessary, without consulting with God's mouth, the examples of the Israelites, deceived hereby through the Gibeonites, and of Saul, whose intention seemed good and necessary, and of Josiah also, who for great considerations was moved for the defence of true religion and his people, to fight against Pharaoh Necho, king of Egypt, may sufficiently admonish us.

Josh. 9:14

1 Sam. 13:11

2 Chron. 35:20

Last of all (most gracious Queen) for the advancement of this building and rearing up of the work, two things are necessary, First, that we have a lively and steadfast faith in Christ Jesus, who must dwell in our hearts, as the only means and assurance of our salvation; for he is the ladder that reaches from the earth to heaven; he lifts up his church and sets it in the heavenly places; he makes us lively stones and builds us upon himself; he joins us to himself as the members of his body to the head; yea he makes himself and his church one Christ.

The setting up of the building.

Eph. 3:17

Gen. 28:12
John 1:51

1 Pet. 2:5

1 Cor. 12:12

The next is, that our faith bring forth good fruits, so that our godly conversation may serve as a witness to confirm our election, and be an example to all others to walk as appertains to the vocation whereunto they are called, lest the Word of God be evil spoken of, and this building be stayed to grow up to a just height, which cannot be without the great provocation of God's

2 Pet. 1:10

Eph. 4:1
Rom. 2:12
[24?]

just vengeance and discouraging of many thousands through all the world, if they should see that our life were not holy and agreeable to our profession. For the eyes of all that fear God in all *1 Thess.* 1:7 places behold your countries as an example to all that believe, and the prayers of all the godly at all times are directed to God for the preservation of your majesty. For considering God's wonderful mercies toward you at all seasons, who has pulled you out of the mouth of the lions, and how that *2 Tim.* 3:15 from your youth you have been brought up in the Holy Scriptures, the hope of all men is so increased, that they cannot but look that God should bring to pass some wonderful work by your grace to the universal comfort of his church. Therefore even above strength you must show yourself strong and bold in God's matters; and though Satan lay all his power and craft together to hurt and hinder the Lord's building, yet be assured that God will fight from heaven against *Rev.* 12:9 this great dragon, the ancient serpent, which is called the devil and Satan, till he have accomplished the whole work and made his church *Eph.* 5:27 glorious to himself, without spot or wrinkle. For albeit all other kingdoms and monarchies, as the Babylonians, Persians, Grecians and Romans have fallen and taken end, yet the church of Christ, even under the cross, has from the beginning of the world been victorious, and shall be everlastingly.

Truth it is that sometime it seems to be shadowed with a cloud, or driven with a stormy persecution, yet suddenly the beams of Christ, the sun of justice, shine and bring it to light and liberty. If for a time it lie covered with ashes, yet it is quickly kindled again by the wind of God's Spirit; though it seem drowned in the sea, or parched and pined [languishing] in the wilderness, yet God gives ever good success, for he punishes the enemies, and delivers his, nourishes them and still preserves them under his wings.

This Lord of lords and King of kings who has ever defended his, strengthen, comfort and preserve your majesty, that you may be able to build up the ruins of God's house to his glory, the discharge of your conscience, and to the comfort of all them that love the coming of Christ Jesus our Lord.

From Geneva,
10 April, 1560

TO OUR BELOVED IN THE LORD,
THE BRETHREN OF ENGLAND, SCOTLAND, IRELAND, &c.

*Grace, mercy and peace,
through Christ Jesus.*

BESIDES the manifold and continual benefits which Almighty God bestows upon us, both corporal and spiritual, we are especially bound (dear brethren) to give him thanks without ceasing for his great grace and unspeakable mercies, in that it has pleased him to call us unto this marvellous light of his gospel, and mercifully to regard us after so horrible backsliding and falling away from Christ to Antichrist, from light to darkness, from the living God to dumb and dead idols, and that after so cruel murder of God's saints as, alas, has been among us, we are not altogether cast off, as were the Israelites and many others for the like, or not so manifest wickedness, but received again to grace with most evident signs and tokens of God's special love and favour.

To the intent therefore that we may not be unmindful of these great mercies, but seek by all means (according to our duty) to be thankful for the same, it behoves us so to walk in his fear and love that all the days of our life we may procure the glory of his holy name.

Now forasmuch as this thing chiefly is attained by the knowledge and practising of the Word of God (which is the light to our paths, the key of the kingdom of heaven, our comfort in affliction, our shield and sword against Satan, the school of all wisdom, the glass wherein we behold God's face, the testimony of his favour, and the only food and nourishment of our souls) we thought that we could bestow our labours and study in nothing which could be more acceptable to God and comfortable to his church than in the translating of the Holy Scriptures into our native tongue; the which thing, albeit that divers heretofore have endeavoured to achieve, yet, considering the infancy of those times and imperfect knowledge of the tongues [languages], in respect of this ripe age and clear light which God has now revealed, the translations required greatly to be perused and reformed.

Not that we vindicate [claim] anything to ourselves above the least of our brethren (for God knows with what fear and trembling we have been now, for the space of two years and more, day and night occupied herein) but being earnestly desired, and by divers, whose learning and godliness we reverence, exhorted, and also encouraged by the ready wills of such whose hearts God likewise touched, not to spare any charges for the furtherance of such a benefit and favour of God toward his church (though the time then was most dangerous and the persecution sharp and furious) we submitted ourselves at length to their godly judgments, and seeing the great opportunity and occasions which God presented unto us in this church, by reason of so many godly and learned men and such diversities of translations in divers languages, we undertook this great and wonderful work (with all reverence, as in the presence of God, as intreating [dealing with] the Word of God, whereunto we think ourselves insufficient) which now God, according to his divine providence and mercy, has directed to a most prosperous end. And this we may with good conscience protest, that we have in every point and word, according to the measure of that knowledge which it pleased Almighty God to give us, faithfully rendered the text, and in all hard places most sincerely expounded the same. For God is our witness that we have by all means endeavoured to set forth the purity of the Word and the right sense of the Holy Ghost for the edifying of the brethren in faith and charity . . .[1]

Therefore, as brethren that are partakers of the same hope of salvation with us, we beseech you that this rich pearl and inestimable treasure may not be offered in vain, but as sent from God to the people of God, for the increase of his kingdom, the comfort of his church, and discharge of our conscience whom it has pleased him to raise up for this purpose, so you would willingly receive the Word of God, earnestly study it and in all your life practise it, that you may now appear indeed to be the people of God, not walking any more according to this world, but in the fruits of the Spirit, that God in us may be fully glorified through Christ Jesus our Lord, who lives and reigns for ever. Amen.

From Geneva,
10 April, 1560

[1] At this point, the translators go on to explain the system of marginal notes and corresponding marks in the text which they have used in the body of their work. We have omitted these explanations as not relevant to the prologues reproduced in this book. (Ed.)

The Prologues

THE FIRST BOOK OF MOSES, CALLED
GENESIS[1]

The Argument

MOSES in effect declares the things[2] which are here chiefly to be considered: *First*, that the world, and all things therein, were created by God, and that man, being placed in this great tabernacle of the world to behold God's wonderful works, and to praise his name for the infinite graces wherewith he had endued him, fell willingly from God through disobedience; who yet for his own mercies' sake restored him to life, and confirmed him in the same by his promise of Christ to come, by whom he should overcome Satan, death and hell.

Secondly, that the wicked, unmindful of God's most excellent benefits, remained still in their wickedness, and so falling most horribly from sin to sin, provoked God (who by his preachers called them continually to repentance) at length to destroy the whole world.

Thirdly, he assures us by the examples of Abraham, Isaac, Jacob, and the rest of the Patriarchs, that his mercies never fail them whom he chooses to be his church, and to profess his

---

[1] This word signifies the beginning and generation of the creatures.
[2] Later editions of the Geneva Bible amend this to '*three* things'. (Ed.)

name in the earth, but in all their afflictions and persecutions he ever assists them, sends comfort, and delivers them. And because the beginning, increase, preservation and success thereof should be only attributed to God, Moses shows by the examples of Cain, Ishmael, Esau and others, which were noble in man's judgment, that this church depends not on the estimation and nobility of the world; and also by the fewness of them which have at all times worshipped him purely according to his Word, that it stands not in the multitude, but in the poor and despised, in the small flock and little number, that man in his wisdom might be confounded, and the name of God ever more praised.

THE SECOND BOOK OF MOSES, CALLED

EXODUS

The Argument

AFTER that Jacob by God's commandment (*Gen.* 46:3) had brought his family into Egypt, where they remained for the space of four hundred years, and of seventy persons grew to an infinite [that is, indefinitely large] number, so that the king and the country grudged and endeavoured both by tyranny and cruel slavery to suppress them, the Lord, according to his promise (*Gen.* 15:14), had compassion on his church, and delivered them, but plagued their enemies in most strange and sundry sorts. And the more that the tyranny of the wicked enraged against his church, the more did his heavy judgments increase against them, till Pharaoh and his army were drowned in the same sea which gave an entry and passage to the children of God.

But as the ingratitude of man is great, so did they immediately forget God's wonderful benefits; and albeit he had given them the passover to be a sign and memorial of the same, yet they fell to distrust, and tempted God with sundry murmurings and grudgings against him and his ministers: sometimes moved with ambition, sometimes for lack of drink or meat to content their lusts, sometimes by idolatry, or such like.

Wherefore God visited them with sharp rods and plagues, that by his corrections they might seek to him for remedy against his scourges, and earnestly repent them for their rebellions and wickedness. And because God loves them to the end whom he has once begun to love, he punished them not according to their deserts, but dealt with them in great mercies, and ever with new benefits laboured to overcome their malice; for he still governed them and gave them his Word and Law, both concerning the manner of serving him, and also the form of judgments and civil policy; to the intent that they should not serve God after their own inventions, but according to that order which his heavenly wisdom had appointed.

THE THIRD BOOK OF MOSES, CALLED
LEVITICUS[1]

The Argument

AS God daily by most singular benefits declared himself to be mindful of his church, so he would not that they should have any occasion to trust either in themselves, or to depend upon others for lack of temporal things, or ought that belonged to his divine service and religion. Therefore he ordained divers kinds of oblations and sacrifices, to assure them of forgiveness of their offences (if they offered them in true faith and obedience).

Also he appointed [to] their priests and Levites, their apparel, offices, conversation and portion; he showed what feasts they should observe, and in what times. Moreover, he declared by these sacrifices and ceremonies that the reward of sin is death, and that without the blood of Christ, the innocent Lamb, there can be no forgiveness of sins.

And because they should give no place to their own inventions (which thing God most detests, as appears by the terrible example of Nadab and Abibu) he prescribed even to the least things, what they should do, as what beasts they should offer

---

[1] [So called] because in this book is chiefly intreated of the Levites, and of things pertaining to their order.

and eat, what diseases were contagious and to be avoided, what order they should take for all manner of filthiness and pollution, whose company they should flee, what marriages were lawful, and what politic laws were profitable. Which things declared, he promised favour and blessing to them that kept his laws, and threatened his curse to them that transgressed them.

THE FOURTH BOOK OF MOSES, CALLED

NUMBERS[1]

The Argument

FORASMUCH as God has appointed that his church in this world shall be under the cross, both because they should learn not to put their trust in worldly things, and also feel his comfort when all other help fails, he did not straightway bring his people, after their departure out of Egypt, into the land which he had promised them, but led them to and fro for the space of forty years, and kept them in continual exercises before they enjoyed it, to try their faith, and to teach them to forget the world, and to depend on him. Which trial did greatly profit, to discern the wicked and the hypocrites from the faithful and true servants of God, who served him with a pure heart, whereas the others, preferring their carnal affections to God's glory, and making religion to serve their purpose, murmured when they lacked to content their lusts, and despised them whom God had appointed rulers over them. By reason whereof they provoked God's terrible judgments against them, and are set forth as a most notable example for all ages, to beware how they abuse God's Word, prefer their own lusts to his will, or despise his ministers.

[1] So called because of the diversity and multitude of numberings which are here chiefly contained.

Notwithstanding, God is ever true in his promise, and governs his by his Holy Spirit, [so] that either they fall not to such inconveniences, or else return to him quickly by true repentance; and therefore he continues his graces toward them, he gives them ordinances and instructions, as well for religion as outward policy, he preserves them against all craft and conspiracy, and gives them manifold victories against their enemies. And to avoid all controversies that might arise, he takes away the occasions, by dividing among all the tribes both the land which they had won and that also which he had promised, as seemed best to his godly wisdom.

THE FIFTH BOOK OF MOSES, CALLED
DEUTERONOMY[1]

The Argument

THE wonderful love of God toward his church is lively set forth in this book. For albeit through their ingratitude and sundry rebellions against God, for the space of forty years (*Deut.* 9:7), they had deserved to have been cut off from the number of his people, and forever to have been deprived of the use of his holy Word and sacraments, yet he did ever preserve his church, even for his own mercies' sake, and would still have his name called upon among them.

Wherefore he brings them into the land of Canaan, destroys their enemies, gives them their country, towns, and goods, and exhorts them by the example of their fathers (whose infidelity, idolatry, adulteries, murmurings and rebellions, he had most sharply punished) to fear and obey the Lord, to embrace and keep his law without adding thereunto or diminishing therefrom. For by his Word he would be known to be their God, and they his people; by his Word he would govern his church, and by the same they should learn to obey him; by his Word he would discern the false prophet from the true, light from

---

[1] That is, a second law, so called because the law which God gave in mount Sinai is here repeated, as though it were a new law, and this book is a commentary or exposition of the ten commandments.

darkness, error from knowledge, and his own people from all other nations and infidels, teaching them thereby to refuse and detest, destroy and abolish whatever is not agreeable to his holy will, seem it otherwise never so good or precious in the eyes of man.

And for this cause God promised to raise up kings and governors, for the setting forth of this Word and preservation of his church, giving unto them a special charge for the executing thereof; whom therefore he wills to exercise themselves diligently in the continual study and meditation of the same, that they might learn to fear the Lord, love their subjects, abhor covetousness and vice, and whatsoever offends the majesty of God.

And as he had before instructed their fathers in all things appertaining, both to his spiritual service, and also for the maintenance of that society which is between men, so he prescribes here anew all such laws and ordinances which either concern his divine service, or else are necessary for a commonwealth, appointing to every estate and degree their charge and duty: as well how to rule and live in the fear of God as to nourish friendship toward their neighbours, and to preserve that order which God has established among men, threatening besides most horrible plagues to them that transgress his commandments, and promising all blessings and felicity to such as observe and obey them.

THE BOOK OF
JOSHUA

The Argument

I N this book the Holy Ghost sets most lively before our eyes the accomplishment of God's promise, who, as he promised by the mouth of Moses that a Prophet should be raised up unto the people like unto him, whom he wills [them] to obey (*Deut.* 18:15), so he shows himself here true in his promise, as at all other times, and, after the death of Moses his faithful servant, he raises up Joshua to be a ruler and governor over his people, that they should neither be discouraged for lack of a captain, nor have occasion to distrust God's promises hereafter.

And so that Joshua might be confirmed in his vocation, and the people also might have none occasion to grudge, as though he were not approved of God, he is adorned with most excellent gifts and graces of God, both to govern the people with counsel and to defend them with strength, [so] that he lacked nothing which either belongs to a valiant captain, or a faithful minister. So he overcomes all difficulties, and brings them into the land of Canaan, which, according to God's ordinance, he divides among the people and appoints their borders.

He establishes laws and ordinances, and puts them in remembrance of God's manifold benefits, assuring them of his grace and favour if they obey God, and contrariwise of his plagues and vengeance if they disobey him.

This history represents Jesus Christ, the true Joshua, who leads us into eternal felicity, which is signified unto us by this land of Canaan. From the beginning of Genesis to the end of this book are contained 2597 years, for from Adam to the flood are 1656, from the flood to the departure of Abraham out of Chaldea 363, and from thence to the death of Joseph 290. So Genesis contains 2390, Exodus, 140, the other three books of Moses, 40, Joshua, 27. So the whole makes 2597 years.[1]

---

[1] There is clearly a discrepancy in these figures. The years given for Genesis add up to 2309, not 2390. On this basis, the total should be 2516. (Ed.)

THE BOOK OF
JUDGES

The Argument

ALBEIT there is nothing that more provokes God's wrath, than man's ingratitude, yet is there nothing so displeasing and heinous that [it] can turn back God's love from his church. For now when the Israelites were entered into the land of Canaan, and saw the truth of God's promise performed, instead of acknowledging his great benefits and giving thanks for the same, they fell to most horrible oblivion of God's graces, contrary to their solemn promise made unto Joshua, and so provoked his vengeance (as much as in them stood) to their utter destruction. Whereof they had most evident signs by the mutability of their state: for he suffered them to be most cruelly vexed and tormented by tyrants; he pulled them from liberty, and cast them into slavery, to the intent they might feel their own miseries, and so call unto him, and be delivered.

Yet to show that his mercies endure forever, he raised up from time to time such as should deliver them, and assure them of his favour and grace, if they would turn to him by true repentance. And these deliverers the Scripture calls Judges, because they were executers of God's judgments, not chosen of the people, nor by succession, but raised up as it seemed best to God, for the governance of his people. They were twelve[1] in number beside Joshua, and governed from Joshua unto Saul the first King of Israel. Joshua and these unto the time of Saul, ruled 336 years.

In this book are many notable points declared, but two especially: first, the battle that the church of God has for the maintenance of true religion against idolatry and superstition: next, what great danger that commonwealth is in where God gives not a magistrate to retain his people in the pureness of religion and his true service.

---

[1] Scripture mentions as many as fifteen, if we include Abimelech, who is not said to have been appointed by God (*Judges* 9), Eli, and Samuel (see *1 Sam.* 7:6). (Ed.)

THE BOOK OF
RUTH

The Argument

THIS book is entitled after the name of Ruth, who is the principal person spoken of in this treatise. Wherein also figuratively is set forth the state of the church which is subject to manifold afflictions, and yet at length God gives good and joyful issue, teaching us to abide with patience till God deliver us out of troubles.

Herein also is described how Jesus Christ, who, according to the flesh, ought to come of David, proceeded of Ruth, of whom the Lord Jesus did vouchsafe to come, notwithstanding she was a Moabite of base condition, and a stranger from the people of God; declaring unto us thereby that Gentiles should be sanctified by him, and joined with his people, and that there should be but one sheepfold, and one Shepherd. And it seems that this history appertains to the time of the Judges.

THE FIRST BOOK OF
SAMUEL

The Argument

ACCORDING as God had ordained (*Deut.* 17:14) that when the Israelites should be in the land of Canaan, he would appoint them a king, so here in the first book of Samuel is declared the state of this people under their first king Saul; who, not content with that order which God had for a time appointed for the government of his church, demanded a king, to the intent they might be as other nations, and in a greater assurance, as they thought; not because they might the better thereby serve God, as being under the safeguard of him which did represent Jesus Christ, the true Deliverer. Therefore he gave them a tyrant and an hypocrite to rule over them, that they might learn that the person of a king is not sufficient to defend them, except God by his power preserve and keep them. And therefore he punishes the ingratitude of his people, and sends them continual wars, both at home and abroad.

And because Saul, whom, of nothing, God had preferred to the honour of a king, did not acknowledge God's mercy toward him, but rather disobeyed the Word of God, and was not zealous of his glory, he was by the voice of God put down from his estate, and David, the true figure of Messiah, placed in his stead; whose patience, modesty, constancy, persecution by open enemies, feigned friends, and dissembling flatterers, are left to the church and to every member of the same, as a pattern and example to behold their state and vocation.

THE SECOND BOOK OF
SAMUEL

The Argument

THIS book and the former bear the title of Samuel, because they contain the conception, nativity and the whole course of his life, and also the lives and acts of two kings, to wit, of Saul and David, whom he anointed and consecrated kings by the ordinance of God.

And as the first book contains those things, which God brought to pass among this people under the government of Samuel and Saul, so this second book declares the noble acts of David, after the death of Saul, when he began to reign, unto the end of his kingdom; and how the same by him was wonderfully augmented; also his great troubles and dangers, which he sustained both within his house and without; what horrible and dangerous insurrections, uproars, and treasons were brought against him, partly by false counsellors, feigned friends and flatterers, and partly by some of his own children and people: and how by God's assistance he overcame all difficulties, and enjoyed his kingdom in rest and peace.

In the person of David the Scripture sets forth Christ Jesus the chief King, who came of David according to the flesh, and was persecuted on every side with outward and inward enemies, as well in his own person as in his members; but at length he overcomes all his enemies, and gives his church victory against all power, both spiritual and temporal; and so reigns with them, King for evermore.

THE FIRST BOOK OF THE
KINGS

The Argument

BECAUSE the children of God should look for no continual rest and quietness in this world, the Holy Ghost
sets before our eyes in this book the variety and change
of things, which came to the people of Israel from the death
of David, Solomon, and the rest of the kings, unto the death
of Ahab, declaring how [it is] that flourishing kingdoms,
except they be preserved by God's protection (who then
favours them when his Word is truly set forth, virtue esteemed,
vice punished, and concord maintained), fall to decay and
come to nought, as appears by the dividing of the kingdom
under Rehoboam, and Jeroboam, which before were but all
one people, and now by the just punishment of God were
made two, whereof Judah and Benjamin clave to Rehoboam,
and this was called the kingdom of Judah; and the other ten
tribes held with Jeroboam, and this was called the kingdom of
Israel. The king of Judah had his throne in Jerusalem, and the
king of Israel in Samaria, after it was built by Omri, Ahab's
father.

And because our Saviour Christ, according to the flesh,
should come of the stock of David, the genealogy of the kings

of Judah is here described, from Solomon to Jehoram the son of Jehoshaphat, who reigned over Judah in Jerusalem, as Ahab did over Israel in Samaria.

THE SECOND BOOK OF THE
KINGS

The Argument

THIS second book contains the acts of the kings of Judah and Israel: to wit, of Israel, from the death of Ahab unto the last king, Hoshea, who was imprisoned by the king of Assyria, and his city Samaria taken, and the ten tribes by the just plague of God for their idolatry and disobedience to God led into captivity. And also of Judah, from the reign of Jehoram son of Jehoshaphat unto Zedekiah, who, for contemning the Lord's commandment by his prophets, and neglecting his sundry admonitions by famine and other means, was taken by his enemies, saw his sons most cruelly slain before his face, and his own eyes put out, as the Lord had declared to him before by his prophet Jeremiah; and also, by the just vengeance of God for contempt of his Word, Jerusalem was destroyed, the temple burnt, and he and all his people were led away captives into Babylon.

In this book are notable examples of God's favour toward those rulers and people which obey his prophets, and embrace his Word; and contrariwise, of his plagues toward those commonwealths which neglect his ministers, and do not obey his commandments.

THE FIRST BOOK OF THE
CHRONICLES[1]

The Argument

THE Jews comprehend both these books in one, which the Grecians, because of length, divide into two; and they are called Chronicles because they note briefly the histories from Adam to the return from their captivity in Babylon. But these are not those books of Chronicles which are so often mentioned in the books of the Kings of Judah and Israel, which did at large set forth the story of both the kingdoms, and afterward perished in the captivity, but an abridgement of the same, and were gathered by Ezra, as the Jews write, after their return from Babylon.

This first book contains a brief rehearsal of the children of Adam unto Abraham, Isaac, Jacob, and the twelve Patriarchs, chiefly of Judah, and the reign of David, because Christ came of him according to the flesh. And therefore it sets forth more amply his acts both concerning civil government, and also the administration and care of things concerning religion, for the good success whereof he rejoices and gives thanks to the Lord.

---

[1] Hebrew, *words of days*. [Called in Greek] *Paralipomenon*, of things omitted, to wit, in the books of the Kings.

THE SECOND BOOK OF THE
CHRONICLES

The Argument

THIS second book contains briefly, in effect, that which is comprehended in the two books of the Kings, that is, from the reign of Solomon to the destruction of Jerusalem, and the carrying away of the people captive into Babylon. In this story are certain things declared and set forth more copiously than in the books of the Kings, and therefore serve greatly to the understanding of the Prophets.

But three things are here chiefly to be considered:

First, that the godly kings, when they saw the plagues of God prepared against their country for sin, had recourse to the Lord, and by earnest prayer were heard, and the plagues removed.

The *second*, how it is a thing that greatly offends God, that such as fear him and profess his religion should join in amity with the wicked.

And *thirdly*, how the good rulers ever loved the prophets of God, and were very zealous to set forth his religion throughout all their dominions; and contrariwise, the wicked hated his ministers, deposed them, and, for the true religion and Word of God, set up idolatry, and served God according to the fantasy

of men. Thus have we hitherto the chief acts from the beginning of the world to the building again of Jerusalem, which
was the thirty-second year of Darius, and contain in the whole,
three thousand, four hundred and eighty-eight years, and six
months.

EZRA

The Argument

AS the Lord is ever merciful unto his church, and does not punish them but to the intent they should see their own miseries and be exercised under the cross, that they might contemn the world, and aspire unto the heavens, so after he had visited the Jews, and kept them now in bondage seventy years in a strange country among infidels and idolaters, he remembered his tender mercies and their infirmities, and therefore for his own sake raised them up a deliverer, and moved both the heart of the chief ruler to pity them, and also by him punished such as had kept them in servitude.

Notwithstanding, lest they should grow into a contempt of God's great benefit, he keeps them still in exercise, and raises domestic enemies, which endeavour as much as they can to hinder their most worthy enterprises; yet by the exhortation of the prophets they went forward by little and little, till their work was finished.

The author of this book was Ezra, who was priest and scribe of the law (*Ezra* 7:6). He returned to Jerusalem [in] the sixth year of Darius, who succeeded Cyrus, that is, more than forty years after the return of the first under Zerubbabel, when the temple was built. He brought with him a great company, and much treasures, with letters to the king's officers for all such things as should be necessary for the temple; and at his coming he redressed that which was amiss, and set the things in good order.

NEHEMIAH

The Argument

GOD does in all ages and at all times set up worthy persons for the commodity and profit of his church, as now within the compass of seventy years he raised up diverse excellent men for the preservation of his people after their return from Babylon, as Zerubbabel, Ezra, and Nehemiah.

Whereof the first was their captain to bring them home, and provided that the temple was built; the second reformed their manners and planted religion; and the third built up the walls, delivered the people from oppression, and provided that the law of God was put in execution among them. He was a godly man, and in great authority with the king, so that the king favoured him greatly, and gave him most ample letters for the accomplishment of all things which he could desire.

This book is also called of the Latins the second of Ezra,[1] because he was the writer thereof.

---

[1] In the Latin Vulgate it is called *Liber Secundus Esdrae,* the Second Book of Ezra. (Ed.)

ESTHER

The Argument

BECAUSE of the diversity of names whereby they used to name their kings, and the supputation[1] of years wherein the Hebrews and the Grecians do vary, diverse authors write diversely as touching this Ahasuerus [see *Esther* 1:1], but it seems (*Dan.* 6:1; 9:1) that he was Darius king of the Medes, and son of Astyages, called also Ahasuerus, which was a name of honour, and signified great and chief, as chief head.

Herein is declared the great mercies of God toward his church, who never fails them in their greatest dangers, but when all hope of worldly help fails, he ever stirs up some by whom he sends comfort and deliverance.

Herein also is described the ambition, pride and cruelty of the wicked, when they come to honour, and their sudden fall when they are at highest; and how God preserves and prefers them which are zealous of his glory, and have a care and love toward their brethren.

---

[1] *Supputation*: reckoning or estimation. (Ed.)

JOB

The Argument

I N this history is set before our eyes the example of a singular patience. For this holy man Job was not only extremely afflicted in outward things and in his body, but also in his mind and conscience, by the sharp temptations of his wife, and chief friends; which, by their vehement words and subtle disputations, brought him almost to despair; for they set forth God as a severe judge, and mortal enemy unto him, which had cast him off; therefore in vain should he seek unto him for succour. These friends came unto him under pretence of consolation, and yet they tormented him more than did all his affliction. Notwithstanding he did constantly resist them, and at length had good success.

In this story we have to mark that Job maintains a good cause, but handles it evil; again, his adversaries have an evil matter, but they defend it craftily; for Job held that God did not always punish men according to their sins, but that he had secret judgments, whereof man knew not the cause, and therefore man could not reason against God therein, but he should be convicted. Moreover he was assured that God had not rejected him, yet through his great torments and affliction he bursts forth into many inconveniences both of words and sentences, and shows himself as a desperate man in many things, and as one that would resist God; and this is his good cause which he does not handle well.

Again the adversaries maintain, with many goodly arguments, that God punishes continually according to the trespass, grounding upon God's providence, his justice, and man's sins, yet their intention is evil; for they labour to bring Job into despair, and so they maintain an evil cause.

Ezekiel commends Job as a just man (*Ezek.* 14:14), and James sets out his patience for an example (*James* 5:11).

THE PSALMS[1]
OF DAVID

The Argument

THIS book of Psalms is set forth unto us by the Holy Ghost to be esteemed as a most precious treasure, wherein all things are contained that appertain to true felicity, as well in this life present as in the life to come. For the riches of true knowledge and heavenly wisdom are here set open for us, to take thereof most abundantly. If we would know the great and high majesty of God, here we may see the brightness thereof shine most clearly. If we would seek his incomprehensible wisdom, here is the school of the same profession. If we would comprehend his inestimable bounty, and approach near thereunto, and fill our hands with that treasure, here we may have a most lively and comfortable taste thereof. If we would know wherein stands our salvation, and how to attain to life everlasting, here is Christ our only Redeemer, and Mediator most evidently described. The rich man may learn the true use of his riches. The poor man may find full content-

[1] Or praises, according to the Hebrews; and were chiefly instituted to praise and give thanks to God for his benefits. They are called the Psalms or Songs of David because the most part were made by him.

ment. He that will rejoice shall know the true joy, and how to keep measure therein. They that are afflicted and oppressed shall see wherein stands their comfort, and how they ought to praise God when he sends them deliverance. The wicked and the persecutors of the children of God shall see how the hand of God is ever against them; and though he suffer them to prosper for a while, yet he bridles them, in so much as they cannot touch a hair of one's head except he permit them; and how in the end their destruction is most miserable.

Briefly, here we have most present remedies against all temptations and troubles of mind and conscience, so that, being well practised herein, we may be assured against all dangers in this life, live in the true fear and love of God, and at length attain to that incorruptible crown of glory which is laid up for all them that love the coming of our Lord Jesus Christ.

THE PROVERBS[1]
OF SOLOMON

The Argument

THE wonderful love of God toward his church is declared in this book, forasmuch as the sum and effect of the whole Scriptures is here set forth in these brief sentences, which partly contain doctrine, and partly manners, and also exhortations to both.

Whereof the nine first chapters are as a preface full of grave sentences and deep mysteries, to allure the hearts of men to the diligent reading of the parables that follow, which are left as a most precious jewel to the church of those three thousand parables mentioned (*1 Kings* 4:32), and were gathered and committed to writing by Solomon's servants, and indited by him.

---

[1] This word Proverb, or parable, signifies a grave and notable sentence, worthy to be kept in memory; and is sometimes taken in the evil part [that is, in a bad sense] for a mock, or scoff.

ECCLESIASTES,
OR THE PREACHER

The Argument

SOLOMON, as a preacher and one that desired to instruct all in the way of salvation, describes the deceivable vanities of this world, that man should not be addicted to anything under the sun, but rather inflamed with the desire of the heavenly life.

Therefore he confutes their opinions which set their felicity either in knowledge, or in pleasures, or in dignity and riches, showing that man's true felicity consists in that, that he is united with God and shall enjoy his presence, so that all other things must be rejected, save inasmuch as they further us to attain to this heavenly treasure, which is sure and permanent, and cannot be found in any other save God alone.

AN EXCELLENT SONG[1]
WHICH WAS SOLOMON'S

The Argument

I N this Song, Solomon, by most sweet and comfortable allegories and parables, describes the perfect love of Jesus Christ, the true Solomon and King of peace, and the faithful soul of his church, which he has sanctified and appointed to be his spouse, holy, chaste, and without reprehension.[2]

So that here is declared the singular love of the bridegroom toward the bride, and his great and excellent benefits wherewith he enriches her of his pure bounty and grace, without any of her deservings.

Also the earnest affection of the church, which is inflamed with the love of Christ, desiring to be more and more joined to him in love, and not to be forsaken for any spot or blemish that is in her.

---

[1] Hebrew, a song of songs, so called because it is the chiefest of those 1005 which Solomon made, as is mentioned in 1 Kings 4:32.
[2] *Reprehension*: reproof. (Ed.)

ISAIAH

The Argument

GOD, according to his promise (*Deut.* 18:15) that he would never leave his church destitute of a prophet, has from time to time accomplished the same; whose office was not only to declare unto the people the things to come, whereof they had a special revelation, but also to interpret and declare the law, and to apply particularly the doctrine contained briefly therein, to the utility and profit of those to whom they thought it chiefly to appertain, and as the time and state of things required.

And principally in the declaration of the law, they had respect to three things which were the ground of their doctrine: *First*, to the doctrine contained briefly in the two tablets; *secondly*, to the promises and threatenings of the law; and *thirdly*, to the covenant of grace and reconciliation, grounded upon our Saviour Jesus Christ, who is the end of the law. Whereunto they neither added nor diminished, but faithfully expounded the sense and meaning thereof. And, according as God gave them understanding of things, they applied the promises particularly for the comfort of the church and the members thereof, and also denounced the menaces against the enemies of the same, not for any care or regard to the enemies, but to assure the church of their safeguard by the destruction of their enemies. And as touching the doctrine of reconciliation, they have more clearly entreated it than Moses, and set forth more lively Jesus Christ, in whom this covenant of reconciliation was made.

In all these things Isaiah did excel all the prophets, and was most diligent to set out the same, with most vehement admonitions, reprehensions,[1] and consolations, ever applying the doctrine as he saw that the disease of the people required.

He declares also many notable prophecies which he had received of God, as touching the promise of the Messiah, his office, and his kingdom. Also of the favour of God toward his church, the vocation of the Gentiles, and their union with the Jews. Which are as most principal points contained in this book, and a gathering of his sermons that he preached. Which after certain days that they had stood upon the temple door (for the manner of the prophets was to set up the sum of their doctrine for certain days, that the people might the better mark it, as *Isa.* 8:1 and *Hab.* 2:2) the priests took it down, and reserved it among their registers; and so by God's providence these books were preserved as a monument to the church forever.

As touching his person and time, he was of the king's stock (for Amoz, his father, was brother to Azariah, king of Judah, as the best writers agree) and prophesied more than 64 years, from the time of Uzziah unto the reign of Manasseh, whose father-in-law he was (as the Hebrews write) and of whom

[1] *Reprehensions*: reproofs. (Ed.)

he was put to death. And in reading of the prophets, this one thing among others is to be observed, that they speak of things to come as though they were now past, because of the certainty thereof, and that they could not but come to pass, because God had ordained them in his secret counsel, and so revealed them to his prophets.

JEREMIAH
AND LAMENTATIONS

The Argument

THE prophet Jeremiah, born in the city of Anathoth in the country of Benjamin, was the son of Hilkiah, whom some think to be he that found out the book of the law and gave it to Josiah. This prophet had excellent gifts of God, and most evident revelations of prophecy, so that by the commandment of the Lord he began very young to prophesy, that is, in the thirteenth year of Josiah, and continued eighteen years under the said king, and three months under Jehoahaz, and under Jehoiakim eleven years, and three months under Jehoiachin, and under Zedekiah eleven years, unto the time that they were carried away into Babylon. So that this time amounts to above forty years, besides the time that he prophesied after the captivity.

In this book he declares, with tears and lamentation, the destruction of Jerusalem, and the captivity of the people, for their idolatry, covetousness, subtlety, cruelty, excess, rebellion, and contempt of God's Word, and, for the consolation of the church, reveals the just time of their deliverance.

And here chiefly are to be considered three things. *First,* the rebellion of the wicked, which wax more stubborn and obstinate, when the prophets admonish them most plainly of their destruction. *Next,* how the prophets and ministers of God ought not to be discouraged in their vocation, though they be persecuted and rigorously handled of the wicked for God's cause. And *thirdly,* though God show his just judgment against the wicked, yet will he ever show himself a preserver of his church, and when all means seem to man's judgment to be abolished, then will he declare himself victorious in preserving his [people].

LAMENTATIONS — The prophet bewails the miserable estate of Jerusalem, and shows that they are plagued because of their sins. The first and second chapter begin every verse according to the letters of the Hebrew alphabet. The third has three verses for every letter, and the fourth is as the first.

EZEKIEL

The Argument

AFTER that Jehoiachin by the counsel of Jeremiah and
Ezekiel had yielded himself to Nebuchadnezzar, and
so went into captivity with his mother and divers of his
princes and of the people, certain began to repent and mur-
mur that they had obeyed the prophets' counsel, as though the
things which they had prophesied should not come to pass,
and therefore their estate should be still miserable under the
Chaldeans.

By reason whereof he confirms his former prophecies,
declaring by new visions and revelations showed unto him
that the city should most certainly be destroyed and the
people grievously tormented by God's plagues, in so much
that they that remained, should be brought into cruel bondage. And lest the godly should despair in these great troubles,
he assures them that God will deliver his church at his time
appointed, and also destroy their enemies, which either
afflicted them or rejoiced in their miseries.

The effect of the one and the other should be chiefly performed under Christ, of whom in this book are many notable
promises, and in whom the glory of the new temple should
perfectly be restored.

He prophesied these things in Chaldea, at the same time that Jeremiah prophesied in Judah, and there began in the fifth year of Jehoiachin's captivity.

DANIEL

The Argument

THE great providence of God, and his singular mercy toward his church, are most lively here set forth, who never leaves his destitute, but now in their greatest miseries and afflictions gives them prophets, as Ezekiel and Daniel, whom he adorned with such graces of his Holy Spirit, that Daniel above all others had most special revelations of such things as should come to the church, even from the time that they were in captivity to the last end of the world, and to the general resurrection, as of the four monarchies and empires of all the world, to wit, of the Babylonians, Persians, Grecians, and Romans. Also of the certain number of the times even unto Christ, when all ceremonies and sacrifices should cease, because he should be the accomplishment thereof. Moreover, he shows Christ's office and the cause of his death, which was, by his sacrifice, to take away sins, and to bring everlasting life.

And as, from the beginning, God ever exercised his people under the cross, so he teaches here that, after that Christ is offered, he will still leave this exercise to his church, until the dead rise again and Christ gathers his into his kingdom in the heavens.

HOSEA

The Argument

AFTER that the ten tribes had fallen away from God by the wicked and subtle counsel of Jeroboam, the son of Nebat, and, instead of his true service commanded by his Word, worshipped him according to their own fantasies and traditions of men, giving themselves to most vile idolatry and superstition, the Lord from time to time sent them prophets to call them to repentance; but they grew ever worse and worse, and still abused God's benefits. Therefore now, when their prosperity was at the highest under Jeroboam, the son of Joash, God sent Hosea and Amos to the Israelites (as he did at the same time Isaiah and Micah to them of Judah) to condemn them for their ingratitude; and whereas they thought themselves to be greatly in the favour of God, and to be his people, the prophet calls them bastards and children born in adultery, and therefore shows them that God would take away their kingdom, and give them to the Assyrians to be led away captives.

Thus Hosea faithfully executed his office for the space of seventy years, though they remained still in their vices and wickedness, and derided the prophets, and contemned God's judgments. And so that they should neither be discouraged with threatenings only, nor yet flatter themselves by the sweetness of God's promises, he sets before them the two principal parts of the law, which are the promise of salvation, and the doctrine of life. For the first part he directs the faithful to Messiah, by whom only they should have true deliverance; and for the second, he uses threatenings and menaces to bring them from their wicked manners and vices.

And this is the chief scope of all the prophets, either by God's promises to allure them to be godly, [or] else by threatenings of his judgments to fear them from vice; and albeit that the whole law contain these two points, yet the prophets moreover note peculiarly both the time of God's judgments and the manner.

JOEL

The Argument

THE Prophet Joel *first* rebukes them of Judah that, being now punished with a great plague of famine, remain still obstinate.

Secondly, he threatens greater plagues, because they grew daily to a more hardness of heart and rebellion against God, notwithstanding his punishments.

Thirdly, he exhorts them to repentance, showing that it must be earnest, and proceed from the heart, because they had grievously offended God.

And so doing, he promises that God will be merciful, and not forget his covenant that he made with their fathers, but will send his Christ, who shall gather the scattered sheep, and restore them to life and liberty, though they seemed to be dead.

AMOS

The Argument

AMONG many other prophets that God raised up to admonish the Israelites of his plagues for their wickedness and idolatry, he stirred up Amos, who was an herdsman or shepherd of a poor town, and gave him both knowledge and constancy to reprove all estates and degrees, and to denounce God's horrible judgments against them, except they did in time repent, showing them that, if God spare not the other nations about them, who had lived as it were in ignorance of God in respect of them, but for their sins will punish them, that they could look for nothing but an horrible destruction, except they turned to the Lord by unfeigned repentance.

And finally, he comforts the godly with hope of the coming of the Messiah, by whom they should have perfect deliverance and salvation.

OBADIAH

The Argument

THE Idumeans, which came of Esau, were mortal enemies always to the Israelites, which came of Jacob, and therefore did not only vex them continually with sundry kinds of cruelty, but also stirred up others to fight against them.

Therefore when they were now in their greatest prosperity, and did most triumph against Israel, which was in great affliction and misery, God raised up his prophet to comfort the Israelites, forasmuch as God had now determined to destroy their adversaries which did so sore vex them, and to send them such as should deliver them and set up the kingdom of Messiah, which he had promised.

JONAH

The Argument

WHEN Jonah had long prophesied in Israel and had little profited, God gave him express charge to go and denounce his judgments against Nineveh, the chief city of the Assyrians, because he had appointed that they which were of the heathen should convert by the mighty power of his Word, and that within three days' preaching, that Israel might see how horribly they had provoked God's wrath, which for the space of so many years had not converted to the Lord, for so many prophets and so diligent preaching.

He prophesied under Joash, and Jeroboam (*2 Kings* 14:25).

MICAH

The Argument

MICAH the prophet, of the tribe of Judah, served in the work of the Lord concerning Judah and Israel at the least thirty years, at what time Isaiah prophesied. He declares the destruction first of the one kingdom, and then of the other, because of their manifold wickedness, but chiefly for their idolatry.

And to this end he notes the wickedness of the people, the cruelty of the princes and governors, and the permission of the false prophets, and the delighting in them.

Then he sets forth the coming of Christ, his kingdom, and the felicity thereof.

The Prophet was not that Micah which resisted Ahab and all his false prophets (*1 Kings* 22:8), but another of the same name.

NAHUM

The Argument

A S they of Nineveh showed themselves prompt and ready
to receive the Word of God, at Jonah's preaching, and
so turned to the Lord by repentance, so, after a certain
time, rather giving themselves to worldly means to increase
their dominion than seeking to continue in the fear of God,
and trade wherein they had begun, they cast off the care of
religion, and so returned to their vomit and provoked God's
just judgment against them, in afflicting his people.

Therefore their city Nineveh was destroyed, and Merodach-
baladan, king of Babel (or as some think, Nebuchadnezzar)
enjoyed the empire of the Assyrians.

But, because God has a continual care of his church,
he stirs up his prophet to comfort the godly, showing that
the destruction of their enemies should be for their consolation. And, as it seems, he prophesied about the time of
Hezekiah, and not in the time of Manasseh his son, as the
Jews write.

HABAKKUK

The Argument

THE prophet complains unto God, considering the great felicity of the wicked, and the miserable oppression of the godly, which endure all kind of affliction and cruelty, and yet can see none end.

Therefore he had this revelation showed him of God, that the Chaldeans should come and take them away captives, so that they could look for none end of their troubles as yet, because of their stubbornness and rebellion against the Lord.

And lest the godly should despair, seeing this horrible confusion, he comforts them by this, that God will punish the Chaldeans their enemies, when their pride and cruelty shall be at height; wherefore he exhorts the faithful to patience by his own example, and shows them a form of prayer, wherewith they should comfort themselves.

ZEPHANIAH

The Argument

SEEING the great rebellion of the people, and that there was now no hope of amendment, he denounces the great judgment of God, which was at hand, showing that their country should be utterly destroyed, and they carried away captives by the Babylonians.

Yet for the comfort of the faithful he prophesied of God's vengeance against their enemies, as the Philistines, Moabites, Assyrians and others, to assure them that God had a continual care over them.

And as the wicked should be punished for their sins and transgressions, so he exhorts the godly to patience, and to trust to find mercy by reason of the free promise of God made unto Abraham, and therefore quietly to abide till God show them the effect of that grace whereby, in the end, they should be gathered unto him and counted as his people and children.

HAGGAI

The Argument

WHEN the time of the seventy years' captivity prophesied by Jeremiah, was expired, God raised up Haggai,
Zechariah, and Malachi, to comfort the Jews, and to
exhort them to the building of the temple, which was a figure
of the spiritual temple and church of God, whose perfection
and excellency stood in Christ.

And because that all were given to their own pleasures and
commodities,[1] he declares that that plague of famine, which
God sent then among them, was a just reward of their
ingratitude, in that they contemned God's honour, who had
delivered them.

Yet he comforts them, if they will return to the Lord, with
the promise of greater felicity, forasmuch as the Lord will
finish the work that he has begun, and send Christ whom he
had promised, and by whom they should attain to perfect joy
and glory.

---

[1] *Commodities*: advantages or privileges. (Ed.)

ZECHARIAH

The Argument

TWO months after Haggai had begun to prophesy, Zechariah was also sent of the Lord to help him in the labour, and to confirm the same doctrine.

First, therefore, he puts them in remembrance for what cause God had so sore punished their fathers; and yet comforts them if [that is, on condition that] they will repent unfeignedly, and not abuse this great benefit of God in their deliverance, which was a figure of that true deliverance that all the faithful should have from death and sin by Christ.

But because they remained still in their wickedness and coldness to set forth God's glory, and were not yet made better by their long banishment, he rebukes them most sharply; yet, for the comfort of the repentant, he ever mixes the promise of grace, that they might by this means be prepared to receive Christ, in whom all should be sanctified to the Lord.

MALACHI

The Argument

THIS prophet was one of the three which God raised up for the comfort of his church after the captivity, and after him there was no more until John [the] Baptist was sent, which was either a token of God's wrath or an admonition that they should with more fervent desires look for the coming of Messiah.

He confirms the same doctrine that the two former do, but chiefly he reproves the priests for their covetousness, and for that they served God after their own fantasies and not according to the prescript[1] of his Word.

He also notes certain peculiar sins which were then among them, as marrying of idolatrous and many wives, murmurings against God, impatiency, and such like.

Notwithstanding, for the comfort of the godly, he declares that God would not forget his promise made unto their fathers, but would send Christ his messenger, in whom the covenant should be accomplished, whose coming should be terrible to the wicked, and bring all consolation and joy to the godly.

[1] *Prescript*: rule or direction. (Ed.)

THE HOLY GOSPEL OF JESUS CHRIST
ACCORDING TO MATTHEW, MARK, LUKE, AND JOHN

The Argument

I N this history written by Matthew, Mark, Luke, and John, the Spirit of God so governed their hearts that, although they were four in number, yet in effect and purpose they so consent as though the whole had been composed by any one of them. And albeit in style and manner of writing they be divers, and sometime one writes more largely that which the other abridges, nevertheless in matter and argument they all tend to one end, which is to publish to the world the favour of God toward mankind through Christ Jesus, whom the Father has given as a pledge of his mercy and love.

And for this cause they entitle their story Gospel, which signifies good tidings, forasmuch as God has performed in deed that which the fathers hoped for. So that hereby we are admonished to forsake the world, and the vanities thereof, and with most affected hearts embrace this incomparable treasure freely offered unto us; for there is no joy nor consolation, no peace nor quietness, no felicity nor salvation, but in Jesus Christ, who is the very substance of this Gospel, and in whom all the promises are Yea, and Amen. And therefore under this word is contained the whole New Testament; but commonly we use this name for the history which the four Evangelists write, containing Christ's coming in the flesh, his death and resurrection, which is the perfect sum of our salvation.

Matthew, Mark, and Luke are more copious in describing his life and death, but John more labours to set forth his doctrine, wherein both Christ's office, and also the virtue of his death and resurrection more fully appear; for without this, to know that Christ was born, dead, and risen again, should nothing profit us. The which thing, notwithstanding that the three first touch [it] partly, as he also sometime intermeddles the historical narration, yet John chiefly is occupied herein. And therefore, as a most learned interpreter writes, they describe as it were, the body, and John sets before our eyes the soul. Wherefore the same aptly terms the Gospel written by John the key which opens the door to the understanding of the others; for whoever knows the office, virtue and power of Christ shall read that which is written of the Son of God come to be the Redeemer of the world with most profit.

Now as concerning the writers of this history, it is evident that Matthew was a publican, or custom-gatherer, and was thence chosen of Christ to be an apostle. Mark is thought to have been Peter's disciple, and to have planted the first church at Alexandria, where he died [in] the eighth year of the reign of Nero. Luke was a physician of Antioch and became

Paul's disciple, and fellow in all his travels; he lived four score and four [eighty-four] years, and was buried at Constantinople. John was that apostle whom the Lord loved, the son of Zebedee and brother of James; he died three score [sixty] years after Christ, and was buried near to the city of Ephesus.

THE ACTS OF THE HOLY APOSTLES
WRITTEN BY LUKE THE EVANGELIST

The Argument

CHRIST, after his ascension, performed his promise to his apostles, and sent them the Holy Ghost, declaring thereby that he was not only mindful of his church but would be the head and maintainer thereof for ever. Wherein also his mighty power appears, who, notwithstanding that Satan and the world resisted so much against this noble work, yet, by a few simple men of no reputation, replenished all the world with the sound of his gospel.

And here, in the beginning of the church, and in the increase thereof, we may plainly perceive the practice and malice which Satan continually uses to suppress and overthrow the gospel; he raises conspiracies, tumults, commotions, persecutions, slanders, and all kind of cruelty.

Again we shall here behold the providence of God, who overthrows his enemies' enterprises, delivers his church from the rage of tyrants, strengthens and encourages his [people] most valiantly and constantly to follow their captain Christ, leaving as it were by this history a perpetual memory to the church that the cross is so joined with the gospel that they are fellows inseparable, and that the end of one affliction is but the beginning of another. Yet, nevertheless, God turns the troubles, persecutions, imprisonings and tentations [that is, temptations] of his to a good issue, giving them, as it were, in sorrow, joys; in bands, freedom; in prison, deliverance; in trouble, quietness; in death, life.

Finally, this book contains many excellent sermons of the apostles and disciples, as touching the death, resurrection, and ascension of Christ; the mercy of God; of the grace and remission of sin through Christ Jesus; of the blessed immortality; an exhortation to the ministers of Christ's flock; of repentance, and fear of God; with other principal points of our faith; so that this only history[1] in a manner may be sufficient to instruct a man in all doctrine and religion.

---

[1] *This only history*: this history alone. (Ed.)

THE EPISTLE OF THE APOSTLE PAUL TO THE
ROMANS

The Argument

THE great mercy of God is declared towards man in Christ Jesus, whose righteousness is made ours through faith. For when man by reason of his own corruption could not fulfil the law, yea, committed most abominably, both against the law of God and nature, the infinite bounty of God, mindful of his promise made to his servant Abraham, the father of all believers, ordained that man's salvation should only stand in the perfect obedience of his Son Jesus Christ; so that not only the circumcised Jews, but also the uncircumcised Gentiles, should be saved by faith in him; even as Abraham, before he was circumcised, was counted just only through faith, and yet afterward received circumcision, as a seal or badge of the same righteousness by faith.

And to the intent, that none should think that the covenant which God made to him, and his posterity, was not performed, either because the Jews received not Christ (which was the blessed seed) or else believed not that he was the true Redeemer, because he did not only, or at least more notably preserve the Jews, the examples of Ishmael and Esau declare that all are not Abraham's posterity which come of Abraham according to the flesh, but also the very strangers and Gentiles grafted in by faith are made heirs of the promise. The cause whereof is the only will of God,[1] forasmuch as of his free mercy he elects some to be saved, and of his just judgment rejects others to be damned, as appears by the testimonies of the Scriptures.

Yet to the intent that the Jews should not be too much beaten down, nor the Gentiles too much puffed up, the example of Elijah proves that God has yet his elect even of the natural posterity of Abraham, though it appears not so in man's eye; and [as] for that preferment that the Gentiles have, it proceeds of the liberal mercy of God, which he at length will stretch toward the Jews again, and so gather the whole Israel (which is his church) of them both.

This groundwork of faith and doctrine laid, instructions of Christian manners follow: teaching every man to walk in roundness[2] of conscience in his vocation, with all patience and humbleness, reverencing and obeying the magistrate, exercising charity, putting off the old man and putting on Christ, bearing with the weak, and loving one another according to Christ's example.

Finally, Paul after his commendations to the brethren, exhorts them to unity, and to flee false preachers and flatterers, and so concludes with a prayer.

[1] *The only will of God*: the will of God alone. (Ed.)
[2] *Roundness*: honesty, integrity. (Ed.)

THE FIRST EPISTLE OF PAUL TO THE
CORINTHIANS

The Argument

AFTER that Paul had preached at Corinth a year and a half, he was compelled by the wickedness of the Jews to sail into Syria. In his[1] absence false apostles entered into the church, who, being puffed up with vain glory and affected eloquence, sought to bring into contempt the simplicity which Paul used in preaching the gospel. By their[1] ambition such factions and schisms sprang up in the church that, from opinions in policies[2] and ceremonies, they fell to false doctrine and heresies, calling into doubt the resurrection from the dead, one of the chiefest points of Christian religion.

Against these evils the apostle proceeds,[3] preparing the Corinthians' hearts and ears with gentle salutations; but soon after he reproves their contentions and debates, their arrogancy and pride, and exhorts them to concord and humility, setting before their eyes the spiritual virtue and heavenly wisdom of the gospel, which cannot be persuaded by worldly wit and eloquent reasons, but is revealed by God's Spirit, and

[1] The original has 'whose'. (Ed.)
[2] *Policies*: methods of procedure. (Ed.)
[3] *Proceeds*: takes action against, as in a court of law. (Ed.)

so sealed in men's hearts. Therefore this salvation may not be attributed to the ministers, but only to God, whose servants they are, and have received charge to edify his church, wherein St Paul behaved himself skilfully, building according to the foundation (which is Christ), and exhorts others to make the end proportionable to the beginning, taking diligent heed that they be not polluted with vain doctrine, seeing they are the temple of God.

And as for those which doubted of his apostleship, he shows them that he depends not on man's judgment, albeit he had declared by manifest signs that he never sought his own glory, neither yet how he might live, but only the glory of Christ; which thing at his coming he would declare more amply, to the shame of those vain-glorious braggers, who sought themselves only, and therefore suffered most horrible vices unreproved and unpunished, as incest, contentions, pleadings before infidels, fornication, and such like, to the great slander of the gospel.

This done, he answers to certain points of the Corinthians' letter, as touching single life, duty of marriage, of discord and dissension among the married, of virginity, and second marriage. And because some thought it nothing to be present at idol service, seeing in their heart they worshipped the true God, he warns them to have respect to their weak brethren, whose faith by that dissembling was hindered, and their consciences wounded, which thing rather than he would do, he would never use that liberty which God had given him. But forasmuch as pride and self-will was the cause of those great evils, he admonishes them by the example of the Jews not to glory in these outward gifts, whose horrible punishment for the abuse of God's creatures, ought to be a warning to all men to follow Christ uprightly, without all pollution and offence of others.

Then he corrects divers abuses in their church, as touching the behaviour of men and women in the assemblies; of the Lord's Supper; the abuse of the spiritual gifts, which God has given to maintain love and edify the church; as concerning the resurrection from the dead, without the which the gospel serves to no use.

Last of all, he exhorts the Corinthians to relieve the poor brethren at Jerusalem, to persevere in the love of Christ and well doing, sending his commendations, and wishing them peace.

THE SECOND EPISTLE OF PAUL TO THE
CORINTHIANS

The Argument

AS nothing can be written, either so perfectly, or with so great affection and zeal, which is not unprofitable to many, and resisted by some, so the first epistle written by Paul to the Corinthians, besides the purity and perfection of the doctrine, shows a love toward them far passing all natural affections, which did not only not profit all, but hardened the hearts of many to remain in their stubbornness and contemn the apostle's authority. By reason whereof Paul, being let[1] with just occasions to come unto them, wrote this epistle from Macedonia, minding to accomplish the work which he had begun among them.

First, therefore, he wishes them well in the Lord, declaring that, albeit certain wicked persons abused his afflictions to condemn thereby his authority, yet they were necessary schoolings,[2] and sent to him by God for their bettering. And whereas they blame his long absence, it came of no inconstancy, but to bear with their inability and imperfection, lest, contrary to his fatherly affection, he should have been compelled to use rigour

---

[1] *Let*: prevented or hindered. (Ed.)
[2] *Necessary schoolings*: necessary discipline. (Ed.)

and severity. And as touching his sharp writing in the former epistle, it came through their fault, as is now evident both in that he pardons the trespasser, seeing he repents, and also in that he was unquiet in his mind till he was certified by Titus of their estate.

But forasmuch as the false apostles went about to undermine his authority, he confutes their arrogant brags,[1] and commends his office, and the diligent executing of the same, so that Satan must have greatly blinded their eyes, which see not the brightness of the gospel in his preaching; the effect whereof is newness of life, forsaking of ourselves, cleaving to God, fleeing from idolatry, embracing the true doctrine, and that sorrow which engenders true repentance; to the which is joined mercy and compassion towards our brethren; also wisdom to put difference between the simplicity of the gospel, and the arrogancy of the false preachers who, under pretence of preaching the truth, sought only to fill their bellies, whereas he contrariwise, sought them, and not their goods, as those ambitious persons slandered him; wherefore at his coming he menaces[2] such as rebel against his authority, that he will declare, by lively example, that he is the faithful ambassador of Jesus Christ.

[1] *Brags*: boasting. (Ed.)
[2] *Menaces*: warns, threatens. (Ed.)

THE EPISTLE OF PAUL TO THE
GALATIANS

The Argument

T HE Galatians, after they had been instructed by St Paul in the truth of the gospel, gave place to false apostles, who, entering in, in his absence corrupted the pure doctrine of Christ and taught that the ceremonies of the law must be necessarily observed, which thing the apostle so earnestly reasons against that he proves that the granting thereof is the overthrow of man's salvation purchased by Christ; for thereby the light of the gospel is obscured; the conscience burdened; the testaments confounded; [and] man's justice[1] established.

And because the false teachers did pretend as though[2] they had been sent of the chief apostles, and that Paul had no authority, but spoke of himself, he proves both that he is an apostle ordained by God, and also that he is not inferior to the rest of the apostles; which thing established, he proceeds to his purpose, proving that we are freely justified before God without any works or ceremonies, which, notwithstanding, in their time had their use and commodity [see note, p. 75]; but

[1] *Man's justice*: that is, human righteousness in obedience to the law, as opposed to Christ's righteousness revealed in the gospel. (Ed.)
[2] *Pretend as though*: claim that. (Ed.)

now they are not only unprofitable figures but also pernicious, because Christ the truth and the end thereof is come; wherefore men ought now to embrace that liberty which Christ has purchased by his blood, and not to have their consciences snared in the grens[1] of man's traditions.

Finally he shows wherein this liberty stands, and what exercises appertain thereunto.

[1] *Grens*: snares or traps. (Ed.)

THE EPISTLE OF PAUL TO THE
EPHESIANS

The Argument

WHILE Paul was prisoner at Rome, there entered in among the Ephesians false teachers who corrupted the true doctrine which he had taught them, by reason whereof he wrote this epistle to confirm them in that thing which they had learned of him.

And first, after his salutation, he assures them of salvation, because they were thereunto predestinated by the free election of God before they were born, and sealed up to this eternal life by the Holy Ghost, given unto them by the gospel, the knowledge of the which mystery he prays God to confirm toward them.

And to the intent they should not glory in themselves, he shows them their extreme misery, wherein they were plunged before they knew Christ, as people without God, Gentiles to whom the promises were not made, and yet by the free mercy of God in Christ Jesus, they were saved, and he appointed to be their apostle, as of all the other Gentiles; therefore he desires God to lighten the Ephesians' hearts with the perfect understanding of his Son, and exhorts them likewise to be mindful of so great benefits, neither to be moved with the false apostles, which seek to overthrow their faith, and tread under foot the gospel, which was not preached to them as by chance or fortune, but according to the eternal counsel of God, who by this means preserves only his church.

Therefore the apostle commends his ministry, forasmuch as God thereby reigns among men, and causes it to bring forth most plentiful fruits, [such] as innocency, holiness, with all such offices appertaining to godliness.

Last of all, he declares not only in general what ought to be the life of the Christians, but also shows particularly what things concern every man's vocation.

THE EPISTLE OF PAUL TO THE
PHILIPPIANS

The Argument

PAUL, being warned by the Holy Ghost to go to Macedonia, planted first a church at Philippi, a city of the same country; but because his charge was to preach the gospel universally to all the Gentiles, he travelled from place to place, till at the length he was taken prisoner at Rome, whereof the Philippians being advertised, sent their minister Epaphroditus with relief unto him; who declaring [to] him the state of the church, caused him to write this epistle, wherein he commends them that they stood manfully against the false apostles, putting them in mind of his good will toward them, and exhorts them that his imprisonment [should] make them not to shrink, for the gospel thereby was confirmed and not diminished. Especially he desires them to flee ambition, and to embrace modesty; promising to send Timothy unto them, who should instruct them in matters more amply, yea, and that he himself would also come unto them, adding likewise the cause of their minister's so long abode.

And because there were no greater enemies to the cross than the false apostles, he confutes their false doctrine by proving only Christ to be the end of all true religion, with whom we have all things, and without whom we have nothing, so that his death is our life, and his resurrection our justification.

After this follow certain admonitions both particular and general, with justification of his affection towards them, and thankful accepting of their benevolence.

THE EPISTLE OF PAUL TO THE
COLOSSIANS

The Argument

I N this Epistle St Paul puts difference between the lively, effectual and true Christ, and the feigned, counterfeit and imagined Christ, whom the false apostles taught.

And first, he confirms the doctrine which Epaphras had preached, wishing them increase of faith to esteem the excellency of God's benefit toward them, teaching them also that salvation, and whatsoever good thing can be desired, stands only in Christ, whom only we embrace by the gospel. But forasmuch as the false brethren would have mixed the law with the gospel, he touches[1] those flatterers vehemently, and exhorts the Colossians to stay only on Christ, without whom all things are but mere vanity.

And as for circumcision, abstinence from meats, external holiness, worshipping of angels, as means whereby to come to Christ, he utterly condemns [them], showing what was the office and nature of ceremonies which by Christ are abrogate; so that now the exercises of the Christians stand in mortification of the flesh, newness of life, with other like offices, appertaining both generally and particularly to all the faithful.

[1] *Touches*: deals with. (Ed.)

THE FIRST EPISTLE OF PAUL TO THE
THESSALONIANS

The Argument

AFTER that the Thessalonians had been well instructed in the faith, persecution, which perpetually follows the preaching of the gospel, arose; against the which, although they did constantly stand, yet St Paul (as most careful for them) sent Timothy to strengthen them, who, soon after admonishing him of their estate, gave occasion to the apostle to confirm them by divers arguments to be constant in faith and to suffer whatsoever God calls them unto for the testimony of the gospel, exhorting them to declare by their godly living the purity of their religion.

And as the church can never be so purged that some cockle [a wheat-field weed] remain not among the wheat, so there were among them wicked men which, by moving vain and curious questions to overthrow their faith, taught falsely as touching the point of the resurrection from the dead; whereof he briefly instructs them what to think, earnestly forbidding them to seek curiously to know the times, willing them rather to watch lest the sudden coming of Christ come upon them at unawares; and so after certain exhortations, and his commendations to the brethren, he ends.

THE SECOND EPISTLE OF PAUL TO THE
THESSALONIANS

The Argument

LEST the Thessalonians should think that Paul neglected them because he went to other places rather than come to them, he writes unto them and exhorts them to patience and other fruits of faith, neither to be moved with that vain opinion of such as taught that the coming of Christ was at hand, forasmuch as before that day there should be a falling away from the true religion, even by a great part of the world, and that Antichrist should reign in the temple of God.[1]

Finally commending himself to their prayers, and encouraging them to constancy, he wills them to correct such sharply, as live idly of other men's labours, whom, if they do not obey his admonitions, he commands to excommunicate.

---

[1] The marginal note on 2 Thessalonians 2:3 says that the man of sin, the son of perdition 'comprehendeth the whole succession of the persecutors of the church', but makes no specific reference to papal Rome. (Ed.)

THE FIRST EPISTLE OF PAUL TO
TIMOTHY

The Argument

I N writing this epistle Paul seemed not only to have respect
to teach Timothy, but chiefly to keep others in awe, which
would have rebelled against him because of his youth. And
therefore he arms him against those ambitious questionists[1]
which, under pretence of zeal to the law, disquieted the godly
with foolish and unprofitable questions, whereby they declared
that, professing the law, they knew not what was the chief end
of the law.

And as for himself, he so confesses his unworthiness that
he shows to what worthiness the grace of God has preferred[2]
him; and therefore he wills prayers to be made for all degrees
and sorts of men, because that God, by offering his gospel and
Christ his Son to them all, is indifferent to[3] every sort of men,
as his apostleship, which is peculiar to the Gentiles, witnesses.
And forasmuch as God has left ministers as ordinary means in
his church to bring men to salvation, he describes what manner

[1] *Questionists*: questioners or doubters; those about to undergo final examination at Cambridge were called *questionists*, so the word may suggest academic pretensions. (Ed.)

[2] *Preferred*: advanced, promoted. (Ed.)

[3] *Indifferent to*: impartial concerning, not a respecter of persons. (Ed.)

of men they ought to be to whom the mystery of the Son of God manifested in flesh is committed to be preached.

After this he shows him what troubles the church at all times shall sustain, but specially in the latter days when, as under pretence of religion, men shall teach things contrary to the Word of God.

This done, he teaches what widows should be received or refused to minister to the sick; also what elders ought to be chosen into office, exhorting him neither to be hasty in admitting nor in judging any; also what is the duty of servants, the nature of false teachers, of vain speculations, of covetousness, of rich men, and above all things he charges him to beware [of] false doctrine.

THE SECOND EPISTLE OF PAUL TO
TIMOTHY

The Argument

THE apostle being now ready to confirm that doctrine with his blood which he had professed and taught, encourages Timothy (and in him all the faithful) in the faith of the gospel, and in the constant and sincere confession of the same; willing him not to shrink for fear of afflictions, but patiently to attend the issue, as do husbandmen which at length receive the fruits of their labours, and to cast off all fear and care, as soldiers do which seek only to please their captain; showing him briefly the sum of the gospel which he preached, commanding him to preach the same to others, diligently taking heed of contentions, curious disputations, and vain questions, to the intent that his doctrine may altogether edify.

Considering that the examples of Hymenaeus and Philetus, which subverted the true doctrine of the resurrection, were so horrible, and yet to the intent that no man should be offended at their fall, being men of authority and in estimation, he shows that all that profess Christ are not his, and that the church is subject to this calamity, that the evil must dwell amongst the good until God's trial come; yet he reserves them whom he has elected, even to the end.

And that Timothy should not be discouraged by the wicked, he declares what abominable men, and dangerous times, shall follow, willing him to arm himself with the hope of the good issue that God will give unto his, and to exercise himself diligently in the Scriptures, both against the adversaries, and for the utility of [1] the church, desiring him to come to him for certain necessary affairs; and so with his and others' salutations [he] ends.

[1] *For the utility of*: in order to be useful to. (Ed.)

THE EPISTLE OF PAUL TO
TITUS

The Argument

WHEN Titus was left in Crete to finish that doctrine[1] which Paul had there begun, Satan stirred up certain which went about, not only to overthrow the government of the church, but also to corrupt the doctrine; for some by ambition would have thrust in themselves to be pastors; others, under pretext of Moses' law brought in many trifles.

Against these two sorts of men Paul arms Titus, first teaching him what manner of ministers he ought to choose, chiefly requiring that they be men of sound doctrine, to the intent they might resist the adversaries; and amongst other things he notes the Jews which put a certain holiness in meats and such outward ceremonies, teaching them which are the true exercises of a Christian life, and what things appertain to every man's vocation. Against the which, if any man rebel or else does not obey, he wills him to be avoided.

---

[1] *Finish that doctrine*: complete the work of teaching. (Ed.)

THE EPISTLE OF PAUL TO
PHILEMON

The Argument

ALBEIT the excellency of Paul's spirit wonderfully appears in other[s of] his epistles, yet this epistle is a great witness and a declaration of the same. For far passing the baseness of his matter,[1] he flees as it were up to heaven, and speaks with a divine grace and majesty.

Onesimus, servant to Philemon, both robbed his master and fled away, whom Paul, having won to Christ, sent again to his master, earnestly begging his pardon, with most weighty arguments proving the duty of one Christian to another, and so with salutations ends.

---

[1] *Far passing the baseness of his matter*: rising far above the relatively low and humble topic of his letter (the restoration of a runaway slave). (Ed.)

THE EPISTLE TO THE
HEBREWS

The Argument

FORASMUCH as divers, both of the Greek writers and
[the] Latins, witness that the writer of this epistle, for
just causes, would not have his name known, it were
curiosity of our part to labour much therein. For seeing the
Spirit of God is the Author thereof, it diminishes nothing the
authority, although we know not with what pen he wrote it.

Whether it were Paul (as it is not like),[1] or Luke, or Barna-
bas, or Clement, or some other, his chief purpose is to persuade
unto the Hebrews (whereby he principally means them that
abode at Jerusalem and, under them, all the rest of the Jews)
that Christ Jesus was not only the Redeemer, but also that
at his coming all ceremonies must have an end, forasmuch
as his doctrine was the conclusion of all the prophecies, and
therefore not only Moses was inferior to him, but also the
angels, for they all were servants, and he the Lord, but so Lord
that he has also taken our flesh and is made our brother, to
assure us of our salvation through himself.

For he is that eternal Priest whereof all the Levitical priests
were but shadows, and therefore at his coming they ought

[1] *As it is not like*: which is unlikely. (Ed.)

to cease, and all sacrifices for sin to be abolished, as he proves from the 7th chapter, verse 11, unto the 12th chapter, verse 18.

Also he was that Prophet of whom all the prophets in time past witnessed, as is declared from the 12th chapter, verse 18, to the 25th verse of the same chapter; yea, and [he] is the King to whom all things are subject, as appears from verse 25, to the beginning of the last chapter.

Wherefore, according to the examples of the old fathers, we must constantly believe in him, that, being sanctified by his justice, taught by his wisdom, and governed by his power, we may steadfastly, and courageously persevere even to the end in hope of that joy that is set before our eyes, occupying ourselves in Christian exercises, that we may both be thankful to God and dutiful to our neighbour.

THE GENERAL EPISTLE OF
JAMES

The Argument

JAMES, the apostle and son of Alphaeus,[1] wrote this epistle to the Jews which were converted to Christ, but dispersed throughout divers countries, and therefore he exhorts them to patience and prayer; to embrace the true Word of God, and not to be partial; neither to boast of an idle faith, but to declare a true faith by lively fruits; to avoid ambition; to bridle the tongue; to rule the affections; to be humble and love their neighbours; to beware of swearing; to utter their faults when they have offended; to pray one for another; and to bring him which is out of the way to the knowledge of Christ.

[1] The identity of the author is disputed. Many, including Calvin and Manton, identify James, the son of Alphaeus, with James, 'the Lord's brother' (*Gal.* 1:19), while others question this. (Ed.)

THE FIRST EPISTLE GENERAL OF
PETER

The Argument

H E exhorts the faithful to deny themselves and to contemn the world, [so] that, being delivered from all
carnal affections and impediments, they may more
speedily attain to the heavenly kingdom of Christ, whereunto
we are called by the grace of God revealed to us in his Son,
and have already received it by faith, possessed it by hope, and
are therein confirmed by holiness of life.

And to the intent this faith should not faint, seeing Christ
contemned and rejected almost of the whole world, he
declares that this is nothing else but the accomplishing of
the Scriptures which testify that he should be the stumbling
stone to the reprobate and the sure foundation of salvation
to the faithful; therefore he exhorts them courageously to
go forward, considering what they were, and to what dignity
God has called them.

After, he entreats particular points, teaching subjects how
to obey their governors, and servants their masters, and how
married folks ought to behave themselves.

And, because it is appointed for all that are godly to suffer
persecutions, he shows them what good issue their afflictions

shall have, and contrariwise, what punishments God reserves for the wicked.

Last of all he teaches how the ministers ought to behave themselves, forbidding them to usurp authority over the church; also that young men ought to be modest and apt to learn; and so [he] ends with an exhortation.

THE SECOND EPISTLE GENERAL OF
PETER

The Argument

THE effect[1] of the apostle here is to exhort them which have once professed the true faith of Christ to stand to the same even to the last breath; also that God by his effectual grace towards men moves them to holiness of life, in punishing the hypocrites which abuse his Name, and in increasing his gifts in the godly.

Wherefore by godly life he, being now almost at death's door, exhorts them to approve their vocation, not setting their affections on worldly things (as he had oft written unto them) but lifting their eyes toward heaven, as they be taught by the gospel, whereof he is a clear witness, chiefly in that he heard with his own ears that Christ was proclaimed from heaven to be the Son of God, as likewise the prophets testified.

And lest they should promise to themselves quietness by professing the gospel, he warns them both of troubles which they should sustain by the false teachers, and also by the mockers and contemners of religion, whose manners and trade[2] he lively sets forth as in a table,[3] advertising

[1] *Effect*: purpose, and result accomplished. (Ed.)
[2] *Trade*: course, manner of life. (Ed.)
[3] *As in a table*: as though in a public notice or advertisement. (Ed.)

the faithful not only to wait diligently for Christ, but also to behold presently the day of his coming, and to preserve themselves unspotted against the same.

THE EPISTLES GENERAL OF
JOHN

FIRST EPISTLE
The Argument

AFTER that St John had sufficiently declared how that our whole salvation consists only in Christ, lest that any man should thereby take a boldness to sin, he shows that no man can believe in Christ, unless he endeavours himself to keep his commandments, which thing being done, he exhorts them to beware of false prophets, whom he calls Antichrists, and to try the spirits.

Last of all he earnestly exhorts them unto brotherly love, and to beware of deceivers.

SECOND EPISTLE
The Argument

HE writes unto a certain lady, rejoicing that her children walk in the truth, and exhorts them unto love, warns them to beware of such deceivers as deny that Jesus

Christ is come in the flesh, prays them to continue in the doctrine of Christ, and to have nothing to do with them that bring not the true doctrine of Christ Jesus our Saviour.

THIRD EPISTLE
The Argument

H E is glad of Gaius that he walks in the truth, exhorts them to be loving unto the poor Christians in their persecution, shows the unkind dealing of Diotrephes, and the good report of Demetrius.

THE GENERAL EPISTLE OF
JUDE

The Argument

SAINT JUDE admonishes all churches generally to take heed of deceivers which go about to draw away the hearts of the simple people from the truth of God, and wills them to have no society with such, whom he sets forth in their lively colours, showing by divers examples of the Scriptures what horrible[1] vengeance is prepared for them.

Finally he comforts the faithful and exhorts them to persevere in the doctrine of the apostles of Jesus Christ.

---

[1] *Horrible*: In older English usage, 'horrible' does not imply disapproval, but rather awe or fear. The root meaning is 'that which causes one to shudder'. (Ed.)

THE REVELATION
OF JOHN THE DIVINE

The Argument

IT is manifest that the Holy Ghost would, as it were, gather into this most excellent book a sum of those prophecies which were written before, but should be fulfilled after, the coming of Christ, adding also such things as should be expedient, as well to forewarn us of the dangers to come, as to admonish us to beware some, and encourage us against others.

Herein therefore is lively set forth the divinity of Christ, and the testimonies of our redemption; what things the Spirit of God allows in the ministers, and what things he reproves; the providence of God for his elect, and of their glory and consolation in the day of vengeance; how that the hypocrites which sting like scorpions the members of Christ shall be destroyed, but the Lamb Christ shall defend them which bear witness to the truth, who in despite of the beast and Satan will reign over all.

The lively description of Antichrist is set forth, whose time and power notwithstanding is limited, and albeit that he is permitted to rage against the elect, yet his power stretches no farther than to the hurt of their bodies, and at length he shall be destroyed by the wrath of God, when as the elect shall give praise to God for the victory. Nevertheless, for a season God will permit this Antichrist and strumpet[1] under colour of fair speech and pleasant doctrine to deceive the world; wherefore he advertises the godly (which are but a small portion) to avoid this harlot's flatteries and brags,[2] whose ruin without mercy they shall see, and with the heavenly companies sing continual praises, for the Lamb is married, the Word of God has gotten the victory, Satan that a long time was untied is now cast with his ministers into the pit of fire to be tormented for ever, whereas contrariwise the faithful (which are the holy City of Jerusalem, and wife of the Lamb) shall enjoy perpetual glory.

Read diligently, judge soberly, and call earnestly to God for the true understanding hereof.

[1] *Strumpet*: whore, harlot. (Ed.)
[2] *Brags*: boasting. (Ed.)